FIRE YOUR
BOSS

BY RYAN WEGNER

TABLE OF CONTENTS

FREQUENTLY ASKED QUESTIONS

DO I NEED MONEY TO START?

Nope. All of the traffic sources covered in the YPG method are 100% free to use. Once you have some traffic and are generating some income, you will need a platform to host your online course. You can use Teachable, Thinkific or ClickFunnels. They're all priced at less than $100 per month and they offer free trials so you can decide which one you prefer. I recommend using ClickFunnels as it enables us to do everything else taught inside this book, too.

DO I NEED PREVIOUS EXPERIENCE?

Absolutely not. The strategies taught inside this book are suitable for complete beginners. Remember, you don't need to be an expert to create an online course, you simply need to be a few steps ahead of the people you're teaching. If you have some kind of knowledge, you can monetise it.

CAN I DO THIS IN MY COUNTRY?

As long as you live in a country where you have internet access and you're allowed to start a business, there's nothing stopping you from creating a highly-profitable online course business.

CAN I DO THIS IF I WORK FULL-TIME?

One hundred percent! An online course business is one of the most incredibly businesses to start alongside your full-time job because it requires very little labour and you don't need to be working on it all the time! You can create an online course once, and sell it over and over!

HOW LONG DOES IT TAKE TO LEARN THIS STUFF?

You can learn all of the necessary skills to start and scale an online course business in just a couple of short months. Considering millions of people go to college/university for 3-4 years to learn stuff that is of no practical use to them in the real world, a couple of months of learning is a small price to pay, wouldn't you agree?

HOW MUCH MONEY CAN I MAKE?

There is no limit to how much money you can make with an online course business. The exact strategies that I'm going to share with you inside this book took me from $0 to over $20,000 per month (yes, per month) in less than one year. I know of plenty of people who are making over $100k per month selling online courses. You may earn more or you may earn less, but I'm confident that *anyone* with the drive and hunger to succeed can generate a full-time income selling an online course in well under a year.

WHO AM I?

INTRODUCTION

My name's Ryan Wegner, and I'm a multiple 6-figure online business owner from London, England. Through tons of (unnecessary) pain and effort, I scaled my online course business from zero to over £20,000 per month in just over one year. After watching my life change so drastically — which we'll get into in a moment — I've become incredibly passionate about helping other people start their own online course business in whichever field they choose.

What I want to do in this chapter is just explain a little bit about my story, as you really need to understand where I come from in order to gain the maximum amount of value from this book. It's so easy to look at people who are in fortunate positions in various different industries and think that they have some kind of god-given talent or gift, when the reality is that most of them are just like you and I. Once you know my story a little better, you will understand this to be true.

So where did it all start? I'm not going to go too in-depth on my childhood, but let's just say it was pretty normal. An important thing to note, however, is that we were broke as hell. I lived in 11 or 12 houses by the time I hit my late teens. I've literally lived in so many houses that I can't recall them all because I always forget one or two of them. It wasn't until later on that I realised this would be a big driver in my success, but we'll get onto that in the coming chapters.

So fast-forward to eighteen years old, and I realised I was pretty screwed. Although I was pretty intelligent at school, I never put in any effort. I'm talking zero — not one piece of homework was ever completed throughout my 12 or so years at school. I always had this 'I'll figure it out' kind of attitude, although there was no evidence that I was *actually* going to figure it out.

WHO AM I?

I left school at 16 with no qualifications or aspirations of attending college/university and I pretty much spent my days playing World of Warcraft. I'm talking sixteen hours a day, seven days a week. I was absolutely addicted to gaming and the thought of getting a job made me feel sick. I was the epitome of the word 'lazy'. Family members would come round our house to visit and I wouldn't even go downstairs to see them. At one point, I even had my desk next to my bed, so I could lay in bed and play games with my keyboard on my lap.

However, after a year or two, I began to notice that the people around me were going places. Certain people were underway with their university degrees, while others were getting promotions at work and beginning to earn good money. I on the other hand, was still asking my parents for £5 so I could go and grab some fast food to eat while I sat at my computer.

This started to not sit too well with me after a while, but by the time I realised I needed to do something with my life, I also realised it may be too late. I didn't have any qualifications so I couldn't go on to higher education, and I also wasn't able to get a decent job. I began looking for jobs and I quickly realised I couldn't find anything which paid more than £20,000 per year. Every single decent job required some kind of qualification or experience in that sector.

Around this time, I was read Arnold Schwarzenegger's Autobiography, 'Total Recall'. I'm not going to spoil the book for you, but at the beginning of Arnold's journey, he felt a bit 'lost' and ended up joining the Austrian Army. So with me being a young, impression-able kid, what did I do?

I joined the British Army of course.

WHO AM I?

I wouldn't recommend joining the military on a whim like I did, and I certainly wouldn't recommend letting the recruiters put you into whichever job they choose. I didn't even go into the recruitment office with a particular job in mind, I literally just told them I wanted to join and they said "we've got the perfect job for you!" and that was it. I was a 'Communication Systems Operator', a fancy term for a radio operator. It involved working with radios in the back of military vehicles. These guys made out I'd be the next James Bond, but I really ended up being a glorified garage sweeper. Little did I know, they just had a quota to adhere to.

Basic training had a huge impact on my journey. While it's certainly no SAS or Navy SEAL training, it's still 14 weeks of brutal punishment for both the mind and the body. But there was one thing I noticed throughout my training — I seemed to be stronger than everybody else. Not just in a physical way, but with the more cerebral tasks too. When everybody else wanted to give up, I almost took pleasure in powering through. When everybody else was crumbling, I seemed to be able to 'crack on'.

This lit up a part of my brain that hadn't activated since I was a toddler. I suddenly began to feel this self-belief inside of me, a feeling that maybe I had been selling myself short for so many years. A feeling that I could do pretty much whatever I want as long as I'm willing to put my mind to it. I used to get up before everybody else and go down to the parade square before sunrise and just look out and visualise my graduation — or 'pass out' parade, as we called it in the British Army. It used to pump me up for the day, and I began to welcome any challenge which may have faced be during the day ahead.

It was also around this time that I began to take an interest in all this 'motivation' stuff and I stumbled across content by the likes of

WHO AM I?

'Tony Robbins and Jim Rohn. That's all I thought it was at the time — motivation. Little did I know that it was really a seed which took place in my mind which would grow into a lifelong pursuit of personal development.

I ended up leaving the British Army after serving for just under four years. I finally had a qualification, too. I had a Diploma in Telecommunications, which meant that I could leave the military and get a job working with BT or Virgin Media or something along those lines, installing fibre-optic broadband in people's homes. This is generally what Radio Operators did. Exciting, right?

Nah, I didn't think so either. I wanted nothing to do with all that kind of stuff, so I ended up getting a job as a delivery driver. I still couldn't find a job which would pay me more than twenty grand a year, so I had to suck it up and accept that I'd eternally failed at life.

I'm just kidding. I knew by this point that if I was going to get anywhere in life, I needed to start my own business. But I had NO idea what the hell I was going to do, or how to go about doing it.

I was working for a self-storage company at the time, delivering and collecting boxes upon boxes of peoples' belongings. Mainly from students who were starting university or leaving university. Sometimes, I'd have to deliver twenty boxes to a student 16th floor of an apartment block with no elevator. Each of the boxes would weigh anywhere from 60lb to 100lb. I'm sure you can imagine how fun this job was. It's important to note that I was also doing this job for £20,000 per year. That's £76 per day, before the tax man comes and takes his twenty percent. That's how broke I was.

My cousin did a similar job to me, delivery stuff, for a different company. But the difference was, he did it on a self-employed basis.

WHO AM I?

After speaking with him, I learned that the pay was higher for self-employed people than it was for employees, because you didn't get all the perks, such as pension, healthcare, sick pay and so on.

So I told him to see if he could get me a job, and he said he'd see what he can do. A couple of weeks later, I got a phone call from his boss saying that he had a spot for me and he'd like me to start right away.

I literally put the phone down and started punching the air. I was overjoyed. I went from making £76 a day to around £140 a day. However, in order to make that £140, I had to work fifteen hours per day. Yes, fifteen. I left my house at 4:30am and I got home for dinner at 7:45pm. And that was on a good day. I quickly realised that it's NOT all about money, and that this way of life wasn't sustainable. I thought I'd do anything for an increase in pay, but when that increase came at the cost of my wellbeing, I realised it was a really bad choice.

Over the following twelve months or so, I lost almost 50 pounds of body weight. I've always been in relatively decent shape but my partner, Suzie, began pointing out that you could see my hip bones. This isn't a good sign when I usually sit at around 205 pounds. The lack of sleep, lack of nutrition and sheer overworking was taking its toll, but I didn't know what to do. If I quit my job, we wouldn't have had enough money to live. But if I stayed, I knew that things weren't going to get better.

Around this time, Suzie also began feeling incredibly unhappy in her job. She worked in fashion at the time, and she was being overworked and underpaid. Things got worse and worse until it reached the point where she would be in tears at night because she knew she had to go to work in the morning. I'm not sure if you can relate to this, but seeing your girlfriend in tears because of your life situation is something which hits hard.

I was reaching my breaking point. I knew that if I was going to get us out of this situation, I was going to have to start a business. But the problem was that I had no idea what business to start. And I also had almost no time at all, except for my breaks here and there throughout the day.

When I first decided to start my own business, I had literally no idea how to even use a laptop. I didn't own one myself, so I asked Suzie if I could take her laptop to work and hook it up to the internet on my phone. I still vividly remember sitting in my van, rotating this laptop around in my hands like a Rubik's Cube, trying to find the 'on' button. I'm serious.

After doing a little research for a week or so, I came across Amazon FBA. I was sure that this would be the thing that makes me rich, but in hindsight, I was just naive and jumped at the first thing which looked promising. And as we all know, promising 'opportunities' are everywhere online.

Long story short, I put about £1,000 into Amazon FBA and barely broke even. I think I may have lost a hundred or two. This was purely because of a lack of research on my part. I was new to business and thought it would be way easier than it actually was. I was selling pest repellent devicesIf you're in business to make a quick buck, just give up now because it's going to be way too difficult for you.

Once I failed with Amazon, I was immediately searching for my new idea. This time, I decided to start a physical products business. This was it. I was about to get freaking rich.

I started a business selling greetings cards. Rude and funny greetings cards for all different occasions. I learned more with this venture than I did with the Amazon thing, because it required me to learn new skills, such as setting up an online store and outsourcing things like graphic design. The Amazon thing really didn't teach me anything at all, other than the fact that I had grossly underestimated how tough it was going to be to start a business.

The greetings card business was really fun, but once I'd made the card and shipped it, I was making around £2 profit per card. So to even make a full-time income, I would have had to make fifty sales a day, and that was just using free traffic from Instagram, which required a lot of work — posting, liking pictures, following people and so on.

I realised that if I was going to make any money selling products online, it was a non-negotiable for me to learn to advertise. It was absolutely necessary. If you don't know how to get traffic to your product, it doesn't matter how good it is. If nobody sees the product, you will never make any money.

But these £2 margins didn't leave me with much room for error, even if I did learn to advertise. So while I began studying the art of Facebook Ads, I decided to leave this business idea behind and find something with slightly higher profit margins.

I began looking into blogging, and this is where things began to get fun. This opened a whole new world of marketing to me as a complete newbie — I was learning about creating digital products, affiliate marketing, email marketing and even some Facebook Messenger stuff using chatbots.

This project was the first one which really belonged to both of us. The first two were just me, but Suzie got involved in this one. We started a health and wellness blog and published articles on how to lose weight and exercise. After a while, we created a weight loss program and began to sell it for $37.

After a bit of consistency, we began to actually make sales. Nothing crazy, only a sale every few days or so, but this was still awesome. It kind of confirmed in our minds that you can actually make a living online, although we hadn't 'cracked the code' just yet.

We began to make a few hundred dollars a month, which was amazing but not enough to allow us to quit our jobs and give us the lifestyle we dreamed off. And there were two main reasons for this: we were using Pinterest as our traffic source which wasn't giving us enough traffic to make substantial sales, and we weren't using sales funnels (more on this later) to sell our products and maximise profits. In hindsight, we could've made a lot more profit if we rectified those two things. But once again, this was a learning experience.

I learned that Pinterest isn't the best traffic source to use, and that blogging wasn't the best platform to produce content on. Nevertheless, I went and studied advertising and sales funnels like my life depended on it. I used to literally watch and listen to a minimum of 10 hours of training videos every single day while I was driving — so this definitely began to add up! Before long, I had an epiphany...

While I was studying all of this stuff and trying to figure out how to sell my own product, I suddenly thought 'why don't I just go to businesses that are already established and set this stuff up for them?'. This was a game-changing thought for me.

I knew how to advertise. I knew how to collect leads. I knew how to do email marketing. I knew how to do all of this stuff. I didn't have a proven product or anything high-ticket to sell, but I knew all of the processes and I was confident that I could help a business make money. So my plan was to start a marketing agency and take on a few clients so I could generate a full-time income and get out of my 75 hour-a-week job — and that's exactly what I did.

I began to absolutely hammer the phone on my breaks and I managed to sign 3 clients in the first couple of weeks. After generating results for these clients, I was well on my way. I quit my job immediately and I got Suzie on board to help me with the admin-related stuff.

We continued to grow the business and ended up signing a bunch of clients, including various companies in the UK and US, a holiday resort and a real-estate company in Australia, and even a yoga studio in Bali. We were rocking.

However, what we quickly realised was that the whole 'social media marketing' business model takes up a hell of a lot of time when you're creating content for businesses and posting on their profiles and things like that. And the crazy thing is, those are the ones that pay you the least. We took a step back and realised that all the businesses which paid the most were the ones who simply wanted us to run their advertising and bring them leads.

So this is what we focused on, and that's where things really took off. We increased our income while taking our working hours from about ten hours per day down to about two hours per day. This gave us tremendous freedom and enabled us to live life the way we really wanted. Over the next year or so, we travelled to more than ten countries and saw some cultures we only ever dreamed of seeing.

Around this time, I had two or three people asking me if I had a course on how to sign clients. At the time, I had no idea what an online course even was, but these people said that if I had a course explaining how I signed clients, they'd buy it. So over the next couple of weeks, I packaged up all of the strategies I used to grow my advertising business into an online course and named it 'The Lead Generation Blueprint'.

The Lead Generation Blueprint is a program that I still sell today, and the feedback has been absolutely phenomenal. Out of over 500 students who have enrolled in the program, I've had three people ask for a refund. Three. That's a 0.6% refund rate. Industry standard refund rates can be anywhere from 7-15%. This taught that by offering a good product, you will make more money. It's not just about making sales, it's also about making sure your students and customers are satisfied with the product or service.

The next few months were the real game-changers. I was making a solid full-time income from providing marketing services to businesses but the online course thing just started to take off. I couldn't believe how scalable it was. As people caught on, I began making more and more sales every single month while not doing ANY extra work. This is the beauty of an online course. It doesn't physically exist. You don't need to buy stock. You don't need to deliver it. You don't need to repeatedly teach it. You don't lift a finger.

As of March 2019, The Lead Generation Blueprint alone has broken the $24,000 per month mark. That's pretty much what I made throughout the entire year of 2017.

So inside this book, my plan is to explain the process I used in order to get myself out of my old position, and into this new, much better situation. I truly believe that this is something that anyone can do. And this is great news for anyone who is struggling at the moment, as it means all hope is not lost!

But before we get into the more technical stuff, what I'd like to do is share some key principles with you which I've discovered along the way. These principals are even more important than the technical knowledge — with these principles, you will become successful in anything you decide to do. But without them, no amount of technical knowledge or skill will work for you.

PRINCIPLES

IT'S ALL YOUR FAULT.

This may sound harsh but it's incredibly true. Facing up to this fact is THE most important thing you will ever do if you want to be successful in any walk of life.

Another way of wording this would be to say that you are responsible for everything. The good, the bad - everything. Once you realise this, you're opening yourself up to a whole new realm of opportunity. It may initially seem quite scary to think that everything in your life is your own responsibility but it's actually the opposite — it's liberating.

You see, no matter how bad your situation is, if you are aware that it's your responsibility and that you are in charge, you will be able to claw your way back. However, if you try and put the blame on something else, you are surrendering power and accepting defeat. Don't let this victim mentality get ahold of you.

Whether you're in an awesome situation at the moment or a dire one, just know that it's YOU who's in charge. Besides, this makes it even more rewarding when you succeed... because it was YOU who did it. Nobody gave you a damn thing.

I take this concept to such an extreme that if I was hit by a drunk driver and severely injured, I would be sat in the hospital bed, kicking myself, wondering why the hell I put myself in a situation where I could be struck by a drunk driver.

The moment you lose responsibility is the moment you lose power. And we all want to be in the power position, right?

HOW YOU DO ANYTHING IS HOW YOU DO EVERYTHING

Another immensely valuable thing that I've learned is that how you do one thing is how you do everything most of the time.

People don't usually excel at one thing and then slack off with everything else. When you meet someone who's absolutely crushing it in life, the chances are that they have everything else in check, too. If they're killing it in business, they're probably handling their money well. They're probably organised. They probably take care of their health and value their relationships. Their car is tidy and their house is tidy. It's a standard they have for themselves.

This isn't always the case - but I'd say it applies in 99 percent of cases. You can only be truly successful if you have all bases covered. If you make a million dollars a year but you're 100lb overweight, you're not successful. The reverse is also true.

Success is about setting standards in all areas of life and meeting them. If somebody has low standards in one area, they probably have low standards in most areas. Let me give you an example...

I was once looking to take somebody on for my business as an assistant, so I asked them to come to my office so I could speak with them regarding their experience and interests. Once they arrived, I had somebody go down and check the person's car.

Inside their car, we found McDonalds wrappers, empty starbucks cups and a bunch of other garbage which quite simply shouldn't be there. Now, if this is how that person treats their car, how do you think they treat their workspace? Or their home? Or their life in general? Needless to say, the person wasn't hired.

SET GOALS AND SUCCEED

The number one factor in a person's success or failure is goal setting. But here's a crazy statistic: the percentage of people who set goals and the percentage of people who become financially independent are exactly the same — five percent. It's no coincidence that the population of these two groups are basically the exact same individuals.

Look at it this way, going through your life with no goals is like sending a ship out to sea with no destination, no captain and no crew. There is pretty much a zero percent chance that the ship is going to end up anywhere worthwhile. The exact same is true with human beings.

Goals give you direction. Regardless of your current position in life, if you set goals, you have an aiming point. You have a destination. And because of this, your thoughts and actions throughout the day will be those which move you towards your goals.

Also, goals pull you forward. Most people just drift through life, day-by-day, expecting motivation to simply come out of nowhere. But how do you expect to be motivated if you don't even have a clue what you want to achieve in life? Motivation and goals aren't two separate things; they come hand-in-hand. The goals you're striving for are the source of your motivation.

When you have worthwhile goals which excite you, you no longer need to drag yourself through the day. You'll find yourself waking up before your alarm even goes off. When this happens, you're well on your way to achieving whatever you set out to achieve.

Another thing to note is that you shouldn't be conservative when you're planning your goals. Let your imagination run wild. Something which may seem outrageously unrealistic right now might not seem quite so crazy this time next year, especially when you begin to realise how much quicker you'll progress through life once you have something to aim for.

When you have specific goals to go after, you'll notice that you make progress ten times quicker than you did when you had no goals — and that's no exaggeration.

BEING BROKE IS A BLESSING

Have you ever heard people talk about the 'immigrant edge'? It's a concept which implies that because immigrants are coming from a poor place into a land of opportunity, they're more resourceful because of this. Which is absolutely true, by the way. Most of us take our situation in life for granted and find problems everywhere, even when we're living in some of the most prosperous, abundant lands which have ever been known.

But the immigrant edge doesn't just apply to immigrants. It applies to broke people in general. I want to make it clear that I mean 'broke' people not 'poor' people. Being broke and being poor are two very different things.

Being broke means that you have no money. I could go broke. You could go broke. Any successful businessman could go broke, and it's happened to many millionaires. Being broke means you have no money. That's it.

Being poor, however, is a mindset. Being poor means that you don't believe that you can be successful. It's believing that you're hard-up, and that money is just for 'rich people'. It's finding a problem for every solution.

Have you ever mentioned to somebody that you're thinking of starting your own business or a similar venture, and the person has said "you know starting a business is expensive, right?" or "that market is saturated, you're never going to make that work."

You know the type of people I mean. This is a poor mindset. Being poor means that you think your life is guided by exterior forces; by circumstance. Being poor and being broke are nothing alike. Financially, you could completely wipe a millionaire out and it wouldn't be very long before they'd become a millionaire again. This can even happen several times over. This is because although they became broke for a while, they were never poor.

Anyway, back to the immigrant edge. This concept can apply to people of all backgrounds, not just immigrants. In fact, I would say that I have the immigrant edge because of my start in life. Because of the fact that I (along with all of my family members) never had any money growing up, I developed this innate ability to be resourceful.

When I first started out in business, although I had no idea what I was doing, I had this strange ability to just get things done. If I needed a logo done, I figured out a way to do it myself. If I needed a job done by someone, I would find a way of helping that person out instead of paying them money.

In situations where the majority of people would say "I can't afford that" or "I'm not sure how to do this", I just found a way to get things done. If I needed a website and couldn't afford to get one created, I went out and learned how to create a website from scratch.

Don't get me wrong, this took a hell of a lot of time and effort, and once you have the funds, you definitely don't want to be doing all of this stuff yourself (as we'll discuss soon in this book). But when you're starting out, you need to be resourceful.

If you're resourceful, you will do amazing things with very little. But if you're not, you can have all of the resources in the world and you won't achieve anything.

If you're just starting out and you're completely broke or have very little money, don't sweat it. Understand that being broke is a powerful thing and you can use it to your advantage, giving you an edge that all of those 'rich people' won't have.

BE A $2 PERSON

I was once on a plane to Malta, a small island off the coast of Italy. I was working on some large projects for my business and I wanted to isolate myself for a couple of weeks.

While on the plane, one of the crew members put out a message through the speaker saying that they're going to be doing a walk up and down the cabin, collecting spare change for a charity that the airline was supporting. The charity was providing clean water to children and families in countries where people were dying of thirst. I thought this was pretty awesome, right?

A few minutes later, a lady began to walk down the aisle with a pot, politely asking all of the passengers if they'd like to make a small donation to this charity. To my surprise, the vast majority of people looked down at their phones as she walked by. I was pretty shocked by this. I mean, they aren't asking for hundreds of dollars, after all.

Out of well over a hundred passengers sat in front of me on the plane, maybe two or three of them bothered to donate anything. I was absolutely baffled. In my opinion, what goes around comes around and it doesn't take much to be generous. It's nice to be nice.

As the lady began to approach the part of the plane where I was sitting, I reached for my wallet. I didn't have much money on me, but I knew I had a few bucks that I could give. I reached around in my wallet and checked to see if I had any coins. After taking a look, I realised that I had two dollars on me.

Now we've all been in this situation before, right? You're about to give something to someone and you're sitting there contemplating whether you should give them more or less. I looked at the two dollars sitting in my wallet and contemplated putting just one dollar in the pot. I mean two dollars isn't much, but I could always just give one and keep the other, right?

And then I weighed the pros and cons up in my mind. I could donate just one dollar — that way, I'd be able to grab a bottle of water when I get off the plane. If I donate both dollars, I won't have any money left on me. But then I had a thought...

If I decided to keep that second dollar, I simply knew that I would take a sip of that bottle of water and it wouldn't be as refreshing. It wouldn't taste as good. In fact, it would bug the hell out of me.

If I decided to just donate one dollar, I would go about the rest of my day knowing that I'm cheap. Knowing that I had the opportunity to help people who are less fortunate than me and I decided to help a little less than I could have. And after all, am I really going to miss that second dollar? Of course not.

So I happily dropped both dollars in the pot and felt at ease, knowing that I've helped in the best way I could. Also, there's a certain selfishness to knowing you've done something good. It makes you feel good — so it's a win/win, right?

Ever since this day, whenever I have to choose between two amounts of something to give, I always choose the higher figure. This applies when I'm donating to a charity, when I'm tipping a waitress at a restaurant, or even if I'm putting some money in a birthday card. I call this 'being a $2 person'.

GET OUT OF YOUR OWN WAY

I truly believe that nothing has more of a negative effect on a person's life than limiting beliefs. Limiting beliefs have the same impact on our potential that a governor has on a car.

Let's say you're driving down the highway in a vehicle that has a governor on it. Your vehicle might be capable of driving at 140mph but as long as the governor is there, it's impossible for the vehicle to exceed 70mph. It doesn't matter how high you rev the engine, nor does it matter how much horsepower you have — there is no way that the vehicle can possibly go faster than 70mph.

Humans work in the same way. You might be (and the chances are, you probably are) a person with 140mph potential. In fact, you probably can't even comprehend what you're truly capable of. Whatever you think your potential is, multiply it by ten, then multiply it by ten again. That's probably somewhere along the lines of what you're truly capable of achieving.

But you might have limited beliefs which are preventing you from breaking out of where you are at the moment. You might have the potential to live a 120mph life but your limiting beliefs are holding you at crawling speed.

The strange thing about limiting beliefs is that they're really not our fault. Most other things are a result of our own doing — not working hard, getting in debt and so on. Limiting beliefs, however, are instilled in us when we're children, before we're even capable of defending ourselves. There are countless different types of limiting beliefs but all of us have limiting beliefs of some sort. The key is to recognise them and understand that they are just that — beliefs. They're not true.

Examples of limiting beliefs might be that you can't start a business because you don't have any qualifications, or that you can't become wealthy because you're from a poor family. Limiting beliefs affect our lives in ways which far surpass just health and business. People have limiting beliefs regarding their own self-image which may affect their personal relationships.

Others have limiting beliefs which stop them from achieving great physical shape — for example, they may come from an obese family, or a family with a history of diabetes. These aren't real excuses for not getting in shape — they're just stories which hold a person back.

It all starts with figuring out what limiting beliefs hold you back and then doing everything in your power to change them. They won't change overnight, but if you stay persistent, you'll eventually notice that they start to fizzle out and their control over you wanes drastically.

A limiting belief that I struggled with massively when first starting out was that I'm not a hard worker. I literally saw myself on a subconscious level as somebody who procrastinates. I never did a single piece of homework when I was at school and I often skipped classes to go home and play computer games.

Then, when I began to get some odd jobs here and there as a teenager, I hated those too. I simply didn't want to be there. I just watched the clock all day and couldn't wait until it was time to go home.

I recognise now that this isn't because I'm not a hard worker, it's because I had zero interest in those things. If I'm interested in something, I can work towards it with an almost obsessive mentality.

But when I first started in business, I didn't understand this. I had such a strong resistance to hard work that it almost drove me insane. My self-talk was uncontrollable and I repeatedly told myself that I'm never going to be successful because I don't deserve it because I don't know how to work hard.

This might sound silly to a lot of people but it just goes to show how deep-rooted a limiting belief can be in one's mind once it takes place. You might have a similar limiting belief that's holding you back, or you may have something completely different. But it's imperative that you identify what your limiting beliefs are so that you can shatter them. Or even better, replace them with more empowering beliefs.

'The only thing standing between you and your goal is the bullshit story you keep telling yourself as to why you can't achieve it.' - Jordan Belfort

IF YOU WANT THINGS TO CHANGE, YOU'VE GOT TO CHANGE

When I was younger, I thought that everything came down to circumstance. I simply thought that my life was controlled by everything around me, not the reverse. I knew that I wasn't happy with my position in life but, as I mentioned in the first chapter, I didn't take responsibility for any of it — it was all something else's fault.

Then, when I was in the British Army, I came across a Jim Rohn video which truly changed the course of my life forever. It was exactly what I needed to hear at that time in my life.

He was describing how he was in a similar position when he was a young adult — blaming the government, blaming his boss, blaming negative relatives. Blaming pretty much everything he possibly could.

Then, one day, his mentor told him that there was one problem with his blame list... he wasn't on it!

He then went on to talk about one of the most profound pieces of advice he ever received from his mentor — and it happens to be one of the best pieces of advice I've ever received, too.

'If you will change, everything will change for you.'

That absolutely blew my mind. If you want your life to change, you have to change. If you do what you've always done, you'll get what you've always got. You can't count on the government to change, or your boss to change, or your negative relatives to change. You have to be the thing that changes.

It's physically impossible to make a 7-figure income while you're a 5-figure person. You literally have to become a 7-figure person — and then the income will follow. The same applies in every single area of life. You can't be a person with ripped abs and a great physique while still being the kind of person who's 40lb overweight. You have to become the kind of person who has a great body.

I didn't understand this when I was younger. I thought that I could continue to be the person I am currently, and then somewhere down the line I'd have a stroke of luck and everything would just fall in place. I thought that one day, I'd make a lot of money. One day, I'd be in shape. One day, my relationships with loved ones (which currently sucked) would suddenly be awesome. Then I learned the hard truth that this is never going to happen and I needed to change something, fast.

I always say that most people die at 25, we just don't bury them until they're 80. What I mean by this is that most people stop learning and growing as young adults. They succumb to external forces and they believe that their lives are shaped by circumstance. This is why some people spend their entire lives unhappy — they're not satisfied by their situation but they don't change themselves. This way of thinking will inevitably lead to a life of frustration and despair.

Take an honest look at your life. Analyse all aspects of it. Then, understand that if you want the areas that you're not happy with to improve, you have to change. Your boss isn't going to change. The economy isn't going to change. Your negative relatives aren't going to change and you can bet your last dollar that the effect that a calorie has on your body certainly isn't going to change.

It's all within your control. Take responsibility and start making the external world morph and shift to your expectations — not the reverse.

PROBLEM-SOLVING IS EVERYTHING

This is one thing which all successful business owners have in common. They all understand that if you're going to crush it in business, you must have a skill or service which solves a problem for others, and that they want to pay for it.

So many aspiring entrepreneurs think that they need an awesome 'idea' in order to start a business. They need to think of something new and awesome which is going to blow people's minds — and that will get them rich.

But this really isn't the case. In fact, if you do think of something completely new and crazy, there's actually a pretty low chance that it'll be something that people want. You might think it's awesome, but it's not you who decides whether or not it's awesome — the marketplace decides. There's a really great analogy for this concept which I heard from Sam Ovens, who I'd like to give a quick mention to so that I'm not stealing his thunder.

Imagine you're in a park, and Suzie is sat on the park bench. And you need to try and figure out what Suzie wants for lunch. Suzie is a metaphor for the marketplace, and what she wants for lunch is a representation for your business idea or product.

Here's what most people do... they just cook a meal of their choice and decide that Suzie will like it. This makes no sense whatsoever, yet so many people do exactly this when it comes to business.

Others might ask somebody else what Suzie wants for lunch. They'll ask their friends or family. They must know, right? Wrong.

Some people will even go out of their way to research it on the internet. But obviously, Google doesn't know what she wants for lunch, either. So what is the best way to find out what Suzie wants for lunch?

You ask her.

It's really not difficult to do, either. You simply go up to the bench, and you ask Suzie what it is that she wants for lunch. She'll give you a straight answer. She'll tell you exactly what she wants — and then you can give it to her.

You see, business is all about solving problems, but you can't solve somebody's problems if you don't know what they are. You won't become successful by creating the next new gadget or app. You won't become successful by wearing a suit and posting motivational quotes on Instagram. You'll become successful by solving people's problems.
In order to find out your audience's problems, all you need to do is go to the place where they hang out. There are large Facebook groups in

pretty much every industry where you can find thousands of people who are all interested in the same things as you. Join five or six of these groups and engage. Speak to people — these are going to be your future buyers.

After you speak to a few dozen people, you'll begin to notice a trend in the problems these people have. You'll see some common themes begin to arise. The people within this marketplace will all be talking about similar troubles.

Then, you simply go out and create a product which solves these problems. If you can do this, you're halfway towards creating a successful business. You still need to know how to get your product or service out to the world (and that's exactly what I'm going to explain in this book) but you've got half of the equation covered.

If you don't know what Suzie wants for lunch, you'll end up creating a product that nobody wants and no matter how hard you push it, nothing will seem to work.

DO LESS, NOT MORE

When I first started my online business, I thought that the more stuff I did, the more success I would have. I even aspired to have multiple businesses in several different industries.

Now I understand that this is completely moronic, unless you're a super-entrepreneur like Elon Musk. I'm certainly not going to tell him that he's doing something wrong. But if you're a mere mortal like I am, you're probably better off focusing on one thing to begin with.

This also applies to the general day-to-day tasks inside your business. For example, when I first started selling digital products and courses, I was putting out a couple of YouTube videos each week and getting decent results. However, I wanted to take things to the next level, so what did I do? I began trying to use Instagram, writing blog posts and I was even thinking of starting a podcast. This is absolutely ludicrous.

Over the past year or so, a huge shift in my business and mindset has occurred because I've realised that you want to be stripping things away in order to get results, rather than adding things in.

If you're trying to do five things at once, you can't really give more than 20% of your energy to each task. If you have one hundred points of energy and you're distributing those energy points between five things, there is no way you can possibly give one hundred energy points to any of them, right?

So with this in mind, why would you try and work on five or ten different projects at the same time? Or even two projects? If you're working on two projects, you can't really give more than 50% of your energy to each project. Even if you focus more on one project than the other, you still can't possibly give 100% to either of them.

Focus is one of the most important things you can have when it comes to starting a business. In the early days of their careers, Warren Buffett and Bill Gates were round Bill's father's house. His father asked them to both write down on a piece of paper the number one most important thing you need when building a business. Without any collaboration between the two, they both turned over their pieces of paper and both men had written the word 'focus'.

When you are working on a bunch of different things, you are literally doing the opposite of this. You're preventing yourself from being able to focus on anything at all. As Confucius once said, he who chases two rabbits catches neither.

Decide what you want to achieve and fixate on it. Then decide on a product or service you're going to create and fixate on it. Then, decide on a strategy you're going to use to sell it and, you guessed it — fixate on that too.

DON'T DO EVERYTHING YOURSELF

When you first begin building a business, regardless of what area it's in, you usually try to do everything yourself. This is because you're not used to delegating or automating things because you've been an employee for so long, and an employee doesn't think about leverage because they work by the hour.

But leveraging other people's time is an incredible way to grow your business. Not only because you can outsource tasks which aren't worth your time, but also because a lot of the time, the person you outsource things to will actually be a lot better than you at that particular task.

For example, when I first started my online business, I used to do literally everything myself. I created all of my videos, I built all of my sales funnels, I composed and sent all of my emails and I ran all of my ad campaigns. Of course, if you're completely broke, this is the resourceful way to do things.

But as soon as I had a little bit of money saved, a mentor told me that I need to start paying other people to do certain things. Now, there are two main reasons why you'd pay somebody else to do a job for you. The first reason is that it's a low-level task that's not worth your time. For example, adding subtitles to a video, or transcribing some audio. Literally anyone on planet Earth can do these tasks, as long as they can speak your language, so you certainly shouldn't be doing them if it takes two hours and you're able to outsource it for $10.

The second reason is because you're not actually an expert at it. I always created my funnels and emails because I thought that if I can do it myself, why would I pay somebody else to do it? Well here's the thing:

you will actually make a ton of money by paying an expert to do these things — not lose money. It might cost you a couple thousand dollars initially, but it's well worth the money if you can double the conversion rate of your sales page or your email sequence.

I thought I was good at these things, when really I was a jack of all trades — and a jack of all trades is a master of none. I soon realised that it's an investment, not an expense to pay somebody to build out crucial elements of your business. As soon as you have a little bit of money coming in, you want to outsource anything that you're not an absolute expert at.

I used to spend two weeks building a sales funnel which made me a little bit of money, whereas nowadays I'll spend twenty minutes on a call with someone who I can pay a couple of grand to create a sales funnel that makes me 100 times the amount that I pay for it. It's far more profitable and takes way less time and effort on my part. It's a no brainer, really. But this is another example of thinking abundantly rather than thinking with a scarcity mindset.

Those are the nine most important principles I've discovered throughout my journey so far. It's taken me a few years to really uncover these concepts and to truly understand them, but once I managed to do so, it made my life significantly easier.

Understanding the principles of success is imperative when you're trying to improve your situation in life. If you begin to implement strategies and tactics without having the foundations in place, it's like trying to build a house on sand. Somewhere along the way, you'll be framing and laying bricks, but everything will be falling apart and you just won't seem to understand why.

Now that the principles are out of the way, let's get into the juicy stuff, shall we?

THE KNOWLEDGE
BUSINESS

THE GREATEST OPPORTUNITY

We live in an incredible time. Never has there been such opportunity for an average person to create wealth without needing any formal education or any kind of special connections. Normal people like you and I can now accumulate enormous amounts of money by simply 'creating' solutions to problems that people are having and exchanging those solutions for money.

The beauty of this is that the marketplace doesn't care about your background. It doesn't care what type of person you are. You can be black, white, gay, straight, rich, poor — it really doesn't matter. As long as you're able to provide value to people, you can create a business.

And I want to make it very clear from the get-go that you don't need to aspire to become a billionaire, or even a millionaire. You just need to decide what kind of lifestyle you would like to achieve in order to make you and your family's life amazing. For some people, this will take a million dollars per year. For other people, it might only take a hundred grand per year. The main thing is just to make sure you don't settle.

I'm not telling you to be greedy, but don't settle either. Don't aim for $50k because you think $100k is a lot of money. You can truly make as much as you want — the key is to figure out what that magic number is for you and your loved ones. Once you set a specific number, you now have an aiming point — a north star.

Now the way that we're going to start this business is by identifying what specialised knowledge we have that can help other people. I don't care where you come from, you probably have some kind of knowledge on a particular topic that other people don't, right? Of course you do.

Maybe you have years and years of experience in growing your own vegetables. Maybe you're a black belt in jiu-jitsu. Or perhaps you're insanely good at doing make-up and all of your friends admire you for how nice you look!

Either way, it's important to figure out what it is that you're good at. And if you're in a position where you're not great at anything yet, that's fine too. Just decide what you're interested in — it doesn't take a million years to develop a skill or knowledge for something. When I first started out, I wasn't overly knowledgeable when it came to marketing but I learned it over the course of just a couple of months and before long, I was teaching it to beginners.

That's one thing I want to point out: you don't need to be an absolute life-time student of the topic. You don't need to be one of the most revered experts in the world. You just need to be better than somebody who is starting from day one. If you have a little knowledge and you're better than someone who's just starting out, you can teach them. Does that make sense?

PICKING YOUR NICHE

I'm not going to speak too much on how to pick your niche, because it's such a personal thing. It makes me cringe a little when somebody's course has a five-hour module explaining how to choose your niche. Just choose something you're interested in and passionate about. I can almost guarantee that if you pick something solely for the money and you have no interest in it, there's no way that you'll consistently create content on that topic for a long period of time.

One thing I would like to point out, however, is that some niches will be easier than others when it comes to actually monetising. Don't get me wrong, you can absolutely make a six-figure income focusing on pretty much any topic imaginable. But there are certain niches which can get you there extremely quickly.

These topics consist of what I like to call 'hard advice'.

Hard advice is information which falls into one of three categories: making money, looking good, and dating. Those are the three niches where you can make incredibly lucrative businesses in very short periods of time. There are various different sub-niches which fall under these categories, and they're shown in the diagram below. You don't necessarily *have* to choose one of these topics, but if you do, you'll make your life a little easier when starting out.

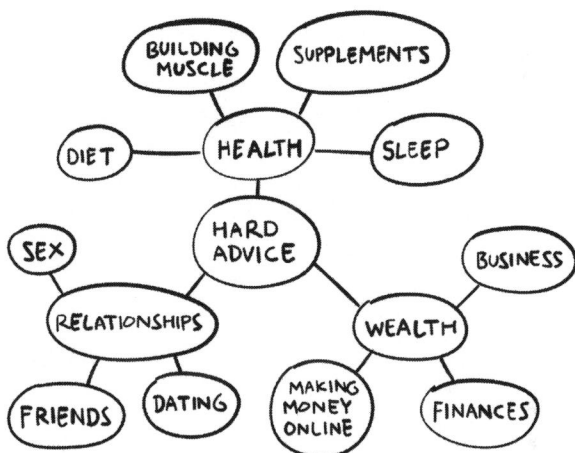

The reason that these three things sell so well is because they really hit people on a deep, primal level. People think that they want to make money because they'll be able to buy things, but the real reason they want money is because they'll have more security in life, along with higher social status.

People think that weight loss (along with other health-related stuff) will mean that they look good, but the reality is that on a subconscious level, we want to benefit from better health overall and also appear more attractive to the opposite sex.

Most people think they pay for dating advice because it allows them to have more sex and appear more attractive to the opposite sex, but the actual reason we want that to happen is so that we can reproduce, which is essentially what we are here to do.

For these reasons, it's very easy to sell people on any product related to one of these three topics. Like I said, you can make an income selling anything, but your lifestyle won't be impacted as drastically if you're teaching people to strip an engine as it would if you were teaching people how to start their own business.

With that being said, if you're not interested in anything to do with those three areas — go for something else. Remember, you're not going to stick with something if you're not passionate about it.

WHY ONLINE COURSES ARE SO AWESOME

There is literally an endless selection of different things you could create and sell, right? But that doesn't mean that everything is equally as good. If you're selling something for $1,000 with 90% profit margins, you're going to make a hell of a lot more money than you would if you were selling something for $20 with 25% profit margins. That's just common sense.

So when you're thinking about what it is you'd like to create or sell, just keep this in mind. If you decide that you want to create a physical product which is expensive to make and has low profit margins (let's say for example, high-quality footwear made from sustainable materials), you're going to be putting yourself on the back foot.

I personally think that if you're first starting out in business and have no experience, there is no better way to get your feet wet (while making some awesome profit) than creating and selling a digital product. Digital products can be quite a broad topic, consisting of eBooks, audiobooks and many other different types of products. However, there's one type of product which trumps everything else...

Online courses.

Let me explain a few of the reasons why creating and selling online courses is so incredible:

YOU CAN PROVIDE TONS OF VALUE

Firstly, one of my favourite things about online courses is that you can provide an absolute ton of value to your customer. It's one thing selling somebody a supplement or a piece of clothing, but nothing quite compared to selling people on a comprehensive course which teaches them, in-depth, about how to do something which could positively impact their life forever.

What this also does is it makes the customer a massive fan of yours, and they're far more likely to continue buying things from you in the future (assuming the product is good, of course).

HIGH-TICKET PRICES

This somewhat links in with the point above. If you're able to provide a ton of value to somebody, you can charge a premium. You can't do this with a consumable physical product and a lot of the time, you can't even do it with an eBook. There are just very few things which enable you to provide the amount of information that you can put forward inside an online course.

While you'll rarely see an eBook priced at over $100, you'll see courses all the time which are priced at $997, $2,997 and sometimes even $4,997. In fact, $997 is a pretty standard price for a course for anybody who has a decent level of specialised knowledge.

That doesn't mean you need to price your course at a four-figure price point, but you should be charging at least a couple hundred dollars regardless of which niche you're in. And when you're making a couple of hundred dollars per sale, it suddenly becomes very easy to generate a generous full-time income.

LOW OVERHEAD COSTS

When starting a business, you're generally going to need some money up front. You're going to need to be able to buy some products, you'll need people to handle all of the fulfilment, and you're probably going to need some kind of workplace to operate from. However, this doesn't apply with online courses.

All you really need in order to sell an online course is the software which hosts it. My favourite software to use is ClickFunnels, as you can use it to build out all of your sales funnels and do email marketing, as well as just hosting the course. We'll get on to sales funnels a little bit later in the book, so don't be intimidated if you're not familiar with what they are.

But once you have ClickFunnels and you've uploaded all of your videos to your course, you're literally good to go. You don't need to pay money when somebody buys it, you don't need to pay anybody to upkeep it — you simply pay for the software. In my opinion, that's one of the most beautiful things about this software. You don't have to fork out a lot of money to get started.

HUGE MARKET

Another awesome benefit of selling an online course is that you have a huge pool of people to sell to. I'm talking the entire world. With almost every other business model, there is some kind of restriction when it comes to who you can sell to. Whether it's a physical product that can only be shipped to certain countries, or whether it's a brick-and-mortar, service-based business that can only service people within a certain mileage, there is almost always some kind of restriction when it comes to the size of your target market.

However, this isn't the case with an online course. You can literally sell your course to every single person on the planet as long as they're able to access it. This means that even in some of the most obscure niches, there are still hundreds of thousands of people ready to buy — because we're able to market to the entire world.

LOW BARRIER TO ENTRY

If you have any creative skills or knowledge at all, you're pretty much ready to create a course and begin selling it to the world. Whether you're knowledgeable on writing, graphic design, music creation, street dance or personal training — there is nothing stopping you from creating your online course.

You can even partner up with a friend (or pay somebody, if you have the money) and get them to record the content itself for a flat fee. Then you can promote the course through your content and reap all the benefits.

Creating an online course is truly one of the easiest businesses to start for this exact reason. The barrier to entry is just so low — there's nobody to tell you yes or no.

INCREDIBLE PROFIT MARGINS

The profit margins of selling an online course are absolutely killer. The reason for this is because they have such low overhead costs, as I mentioned earlier. In most businesses, when you have physical products and employees and so on, 50% profit margins would be pretty killer. If you have that kind of profit margin, you're in a pretty good position to grow your business.

Online courses, however, are almost 100% profit margins. Yes, you heard that right — 100%. In fact, a few months ago, I sold $24,000 worth of one of my online courses without spending a single penny on advertising — which meant that my only expenses were ClickFunnels ($97) and my email automation software ($49).

My total expenses in order to sell my online course were $146. How insane is that? I made $24,000 in a single month and my total outgoings came to $146. That's like 99.5% profit margins! That is literally unheard of in any other business model in the world.

These types of profit margins mean that as an online course creator, you're able to invest more money back into your business than any other kind of business owner. When you're able to do this, it makes life a lot easier when you decide to grow and scale your business.

YOU DON'T NEED ANY STOCK

Another awesome thing about an online course is that you don't need to keep any stock. In any other kind of product-based business, you're going to have to actually 'create' a physical product — whether you do it yourself or work with a manufacturer. This is going to include designing the product, having it created, ordering samples, and then actually buying the product in bulk so that you're able to handle a high-volume of orders once you go live.

With an online course, however, you never actually have any physical product at all. It doesn't even exist. It's simply cloud-based content that can be sold over and over again, with little-to-no additional costs.

It doesn't matter whether you sell your product to fifty people or fifty-thousand people, you still never need to actually buy or stock a physical product. How cool is that?

EVERYTHING CAN BE AUTOMATED

This is one of the most incredible things about digital products in general. Once the product itself is created, literally everything else can be automated. You can automate the sale of the product through webinars and other trainings where you can pitch your product at the end. Then you can automate the ongoing marketing of the product through email sequences (more on that later). Then when people actually buy the product, you can automate the entire checkout and delivery process, meaning they can purchase the product and have full access to it while you're sleeping soundly in your bed.

The fact that this can all be automated so efficiently means that this business model is far easier to scale than pretty much every other business model. There are no bottlenecks — you basically have unlimited stock, your costs don't go up when you sell to more people, and you put zero work into actually delivering the product. It's absolutely crazy.

GETTING YOUR PRODUCT OUT THERE

MONEY FOLLOWS ATTENTION

So we've been over all of the amazing benefits of selling an online course, but all the benefits in the world will mean nothing if you can't get your product out into the marketplace.

Money follows attention. Whenever there are tons of eyeballs on something or someone, you can pretty much count on it that there's also a lot of money being made. Take the Kardashians for example. They don't seem to be doing anything special, other than drawing attention to themselves. But this is something they're really good at. And because of this, they make an incredible amount of money.

Think about how many amazing products there are out there which are failing, or how many talented musicians or actors are struggling to pay their bills. They're literally everywhere. There's no shortage of good products or valuable skills. But if you can't get the product or skill out into the world, it stands for nothing.

Kylie Jenner, however, managed to build her lipstick company to the point where it generated $420 million in just 18 months after it was formed. She managed to grow her company more in 18 months than most of the other top cosmetic brands managed in 80 years. This is the power of attention.

So now that we're clear on that, what is the best way to go out there and market your product? Well, there are tons of ways. Here are just a few of them:

- Facebook
- Instagram
- YouTube
- Twitter

- Snapchat
- Pinterest
- Blogging
- Podcasts
- Audiobooks
- Email Marketing
- TV Ads
- Radio Ads
- Social Media Ads

The list goes on. I'd literally be here all day if I were to list out all of the different ways that you can advertise your product.

Through a ton of trial and error (trust me, I've tried almost all of the methods mentioned above), I've realised that for the vast majority of niches, there's a very specific set of platforms which work best for attracting people who are interested in your products and are ready to spend money on them. This is something that I've boiled down to a science and called it the 'YPG' method.

'YPG' is an acronym for 'YouTube, Facebook Profile and Facebook Groups'. These, in my opinion, are great platforms to use for pretty much any niche, because they're so diverse and also offer fantastic ways of actually building intimacy with your market. Other platforms don't allow you to do this — you can't really build relationships with people through Pinterest, or in an audiobook.

Instagram is a great platform, too — for certain niches. If you're in a very visual niche such as fitness or fashion, obviously it makes sense to utilise Instagram. That's not something I'm going to be covering in this book but I don't want you thinking that you have to ignore the platform. If it makes sense, use it.

RAPPORT IS EVERYTHING

Before we get into the YPG method, I want to explain something very important. Whenever you sell any kind of product or service, rapport is absolutely essential. Regardless of what it is, people buy things from people they know, like and trust. The more you can get somebody to know, like and trust you, the more likely they are to actually invest in you and your product.

Therefore, when we sell something online (or even offline), you can't just go for the kill. You can't just talk about your product non-stop, pushing it down people's throats and expecting them to buy it before they even know you. This is the marketing equivalent of walking up to a random member of the opposite sex and repeatedly asking them to sleep with you. You wouldn't do that, would you? I hope you wouldn't anyway. You need to warm them up first, you know? You need to build that 'know, like and trust' factor.

Now, you can't personally walk up and approach every single person in your marketplace — that would take a hundred lifetimes. But there's a more efficient technique that we can use which is great at building rapport with your potential customers. And this technique is called 'content creation'.

Content is basically any piece of information that you put into the world — period. It can come in many forms — books are content, films are content, songs are content. Any information which people can consume would be considered as content.

But in this business, we're not looking to entertain people. We're not looking to provide them with songs or documentaries — unless that's the niche you're specialising in, of course. What we're looking to do here is provide them with solutions. We're looking for a problem, and helping people to find a solution. That's the kind of content we want to create.

If you can do this, you will be able to build an extremely powerful personal brand and you'll develop massive amounts of trust with your potential customers. Once you are creating content which truly helps your audience, you won't believe how easy it becomes to make money and build a business.

There are dozens of different types of content that you can create for your audience, and all of them can be used on pretty much any platform. What I'm going to do is give you five of my favourite types of content which build massive amounts of rapport between you and your audience, just to make your life a little easier when you first start out. If you go with one of these content types each day, you can't go far wrong.

'VALUE' POST

The clue is in the name with this one. You want to provide value to your audience — teach them something about the topic that they didn't know — try to give them an 'aha' moment. When you do this, you'll build that know, like and trust' factor with every post you put out.

You want to be careful that you don't reveal too much information, though. You need to bear in mind that you are selling a product which is intended to solve the problem completely, so you don't want to give away so much in your Facebook posts that they don't even need your product.

However, with that being said, you still want to make sure that these value posts are useful for everybody they're aimed at — whether they buy your product or not. You don't want to string people along, which is what I see a lot of people do. They post things 'disguised' as value but it doesn't actually help anybody at all, and the only way to really gain any value is to buy the person's product. I really don't believe in this approach and it gets on my nerves. I have paid products which I want people to buy, but people can still watch my free content and put it into action.

Put out free content which helps people with 80% of the problem. Also help people with the higher level concepts and things like that. Then keep the real nitty-gritty stuff for your paid products.

'ADDRESSING FALSE BELIEFS' POST

These posts work really well because a lot of the time, the reason a person doesn't achieve their desired outcome or goal is because they have a limiting belief as to why they can't do it. The funny thing is, this is often the reason they won't buy your product, too.

If you want somebody to buy your product which helps them achieve the end result, they must first actually believe that they can achieve said result. If somebody has very little certainty that they can even start a business at all, the likelihood of them paying a business coach is slim-to-none.

This applies in literally any market. If somebody has limiting beliefs which lead them to think that they're always going to be fat and they're never going to be able to lose weight, that person isn't going to actively seek out a personal trainer.

A great way to shatter these false beliefs is first to address them, then follow up with a story which explains how somebody else in a similar situation overcame this problem. For example, an 'addressing false beliefs' post may look something like this:

"Have you ever thought about starting a business but you don't think you can do it because you have no qualifications?

This a common misconception I see all the time with people who are just starting out. The truth is, you don't actually need any qualifications at all; all you need to do is be able to solve problems.

For example my client, Sally, always knew that she was destined for something better than her soul-crushing job as an admin assistant, but she believed that because she lacked business qualifications, she would never be able to start a business. Little did she know what was actually going to occur when she began working with a coach...

Sally and I came up with a step-by-step action plan which would allow her to build a profitable business selling a digital product which taught people how to dance, which is something she's super passionate about! She learned all the simple skills and strategies (which anyone can learn by the way) that were required and we got to work.

Here's the crazy thing - just six months later, Sally is on the verge of making a six-figure income and she actually works LESS than she did to start with! She's also way more fulfilled and is now able to enjoy time with her family — something she was never able to do in her job. Way to go, Sally!"

That's an example of an 'addressing false beliefs' post. You don't want to 'push' people towards working with you, but if there's anybody following you who thinks they can't get their desired result, you need to be eliminating those beliefs. This is actually a form of objection handling.

'ENGAGEMENT' POST

Engagement posts are great for just that — engaging with your audience. But there's also a hidden perk behind these types of posts. You see, when you post something on social media and it gets a lot of attention (good or bad), there are algorithms in place which will pick up on this and show your posts to more people next time. Facebook, YouTube, Instagram, Google, everything... all of these platforms have algorithms which detect which posts are performing well.

So as well as helping you get to know your audience, engagement posts are a really cool way of telling the platform that your content is getting a lot of attention and they should probably show your stuff to more people.

'PAIN & PROBLEM' POST

These kind of posts are really useful for touching on people's emotions and getting them to consider taking action in order to get out of their current situation. Every single buying decision ever made is done so in order to solve some kind of problem. Some problems are more serious than others, but they're all problems nonetheless. If somebody buys a loaf of bread, they do so because they have a problem — they've run out of bread. Similarly, if somebody pays $100,000 for an operation to cure a rare disease, they also have a problem. They could die if they don't solve the problem. But either way, both things are problems. It's also important to note that you will be paid based on the severity and importance of the problem you're solving.

Anyway, I digress. Touching on people's problems is a great way to make them reason that the problem actually does exist and that they should really think about solving it. Sometimes, people have a problem and they're not even aware of it. How many people happily sit 40lb overweight for years on end without ever even thinking about stepping foot in a gym? Everybody knows that being 40lb overweight isn't healthy, but if they're not actively thinking about it, then they will never take action to resolve the issue.

In these posts, you want to talk about a common problem that your target customer may be experiencing, and then talk about the different pains and issues which are going to arise if this problem isn't solved. Then, when they finally realise that it needs to be addressed, they will come to you to help them solve it.

'CALL-TO-ACTION' POST

Call-to-action posts are awesome. These are basically posts where you tell people what it is that you're offering and you tell them to take action. In our case, we're telling them to buy our course.

You can also mix in elements of scarcity within these posts. Things such as deadlines, a limited number of places, or a time-based discount. These are all things that get people to take action. You can't just say 'hey, buy my stuff'. You have to give people a reason why they need to act now, and also explain how they'll miss out if they don't.

An important thing to note is that you shouldn't use these posts too frequently. Remember what I said before about 'warming people up'? If you use this type of post too often, you'll stop providing value and you'll ruin the relationship you've built with your target market. I'd recommend using pure call-to-action posts only about 20% of the time. If one in five of your posts are done in this style, you'll do pretty damn well.

THE 'YPG' METHOD

So we've spoken about how important it is to build rapport with your audience through valuable content, and we've spoken about a few different types of content that you can use in order to do so. Now, I want to explain how to use the YPG method — why these platforms are so useful and how to use them effectively.

YOUTUBE: THE SECOND MOST POPULAR WEBSITE ON THE PLANET

As of the writing of this book, YouTube comes second only to Google in terms of the sheer number of people visiting the website. As I'm sure you can imagine, this means a LOT of potential customers for us. It's going to be the main platform that we're going to use because it gives us tons of organic traffic, meaning that we don't need to solely rely on sending people to our videos — YouTube will actually show them to people automatically.

Also, another awesome thing to note about YouTube is that it's a search engine. Meaning that people aren't just going there to be entertained like they are on Twitter or Snapchat; they're actually going there to find solutions to problems. 'How to' is one of the most common phrases searched on the platform, and every time somebody starts a sentence with 'how to', they're looking for a solution to a problem. And a lot of the time, the person is willing to pull out their credit card if there's a good enough solution.

YouTube is also incredibly useful for building trust with your audience. There's something about actually being on camera which builds a relationship far greater than a blog article or a Facebook post ever could. In fact, I was extremely camera-shy when I first started out in business, and I was looking for every possible alternative I could use to prevent me from having to get on camera.

Then one day, I just thought 'screw it' and I pulled out the camera, recorded a video and uploaded it. After four or five videos, I began to feel far less anxious on camera and over the next four or five months, I actually quadrupled my income. I credit a huge part of my success online to actually biting the bullet and getting on camera. I always say that when you're first starting out, you should absolutely get on camera because it just makes things SO much easier.

If you refuse to get on camera, you're literally choosing to make it five times harder to make an income online. Bear this in mind before you start saying 'oh, but I'm camera-shy'. Don't worry about what your friends or family think — they won't be laughing when you're making a six or seven-figure income from your business... they'll be asking you how you did it.

When you upload videos to YouTube, it's also extremely important that you effectively optimise your videos for the search engine. This is called 'SEO' — search engine optimisation. There are certain things you can do in the process of uploading your videos which will make it show up higher in the search results, leading to more people watching your stuff and ultimately, more money in your bank account.

With any search engine, it's crucial that you can get your video on the first few pages, with the first page obviously being optimal. YouTube has millions of videos uploaded every single day and 99.9% of these videos are lost in the abyss that is the internet. They get one or two views and then nobody ever sees them again. We definitely don't want this happening to our content!

This is why it's key to properly optimise our video content — so we give it the best chance of ranking and getting eyeballs on it. Remember, eyeballs mean money.

There are some very specific things that you can do in order to give your videos the best chance of ranking. There are outside factors in play as well — things such as the standard of your competitor's videos, whether or not they spend money to promote their videos and things like that. But if you follow what I'm about to explain and you make sure your actual content is good quality, you'll get the result you want more often than not.

Here are nine things that you should bear in mind each and every time you upload a video to YouTube:

ENGAGEMENT

Before uploading your video, it's important to understand that a major factor in YouTube's ranking algorithm comes down to whether or not a video is engaging. What I mean by engaging is, does it get people to comment, like and share? Before you even upload your video, you should bear this in mind when actually creating the video itself.

Make sure you take the opportunity at both the beginning and the end of the video (and sometimes even during the video if it's slightly longer) to tell people to like the video and leave a comment. It's a good idea to ask your viewers a question or for their opinion on something and tell them to leave a comment below.

I also see people running contests where they give away cash prizes or goodies each week, and in order to enter, you simply need to like, subscribe and leave a comment. This might not be something you're able to do at the moment, but as soon as you start seeing some financial success, this will absolutely supercharge your engagement. When there's a couple bucks on the line, you'll find that it's very easy to get people to drop a comment! The more you can get people to engage with your videos, the more views you will tend to get. This means more money for you, so get creative and think of some ways to get people to engage!

AUDIENCE RETENTION

Another major factor in ranking videos is the retention of your video. What this means is, how long do people actually watch your videos for? If people are leaving your video just 10% of the way through, that's not good. But if your average retention rate is 90%, you're absolutely crushing it! This is another thing that YouTube tracks, on every single view of every single video. Crazy right?

So with that being said, the longer you can keep people on your videos, the better the chance of ranking them. If you go on most successful YouTube channels, you'll notice that they always give some kind of reason for people to stay until the end. They will say 'if you stay all the way to the end of the video, I've got an awesome goodie that I want to give you' or something along those lines. They're not just doing this for no reason — they understand that the longer YOU stay, the more people will see their video.

KEYWORD RESEARCH

When uploading a video to YouTube, we need to be very clear on which keywords we want to rank for. You can't just appear on somebody's screen whenever they search any random term — we need to rank for relevant terms.

The way that we do this is by doing proper keyword research. This also ties into the next three tips but we'll get to that in a moment. For now, we just need to know which keywords we're going to target.

An awesome tool that I use to do keyword research is TubeBuddy. It's real cheap — just a few bucks per month — and it allows you to do some really cool things on YouTube. But the main thing is keyword research.

TubeBuddy has a tool called 'Keyword Explorer' which gives you different metrics on whichever keyword you choose. It tells you things like search volume, competition and lots of other pieces of information. But the most useful feature is the 'overall score'. This basically indicates whether we should optimise for this search term or not, based on all of the different aspects of the keyword. It lets us know whether we have a chance of ranking for a particular keyword, or if a keyword is even worth targeting at all.

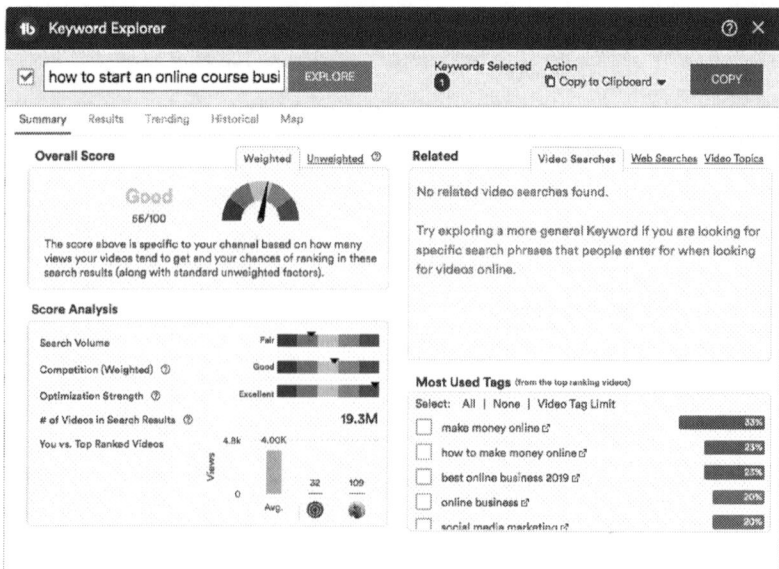

Screenshot of TubeBuddy's Keyword Explorer tool.

If you target a badly-chosen keyword, you'll have no chance of ranking for it and your content will end up being lost in a giant pool of unseen videos. It's crucial to do proper keyword research, else the next couple of steps will be useless.

VIDEO TITLE

The title of your video is one of the biggest ranking factors for YouTube's algorithm. It should explain exactly what your video is going to be about.

You want your keyword to appear naturally in your title, and ideally you want to weave it into a search term which people are likely to be searching for. For example, if your target keyword is 'online business', you may want to have your video title as 'How to Start an Online Business Even as a Complete Beginner'.

Also, it's best to keep your video title under 60 characters. This way, when it appears in somebody's search results, they'll be able to see the full title of the video, as opposed to half of the title. It's been shown that a full title makes people more likely to click on the video.

VIDEO DESCRIPTION

The video description is the area underneath the video which describes (hence the name) what the video is all about. Google says that you can use up to 1,000 words in your description but people didn't click your video to read an essay. For this reason, I'd recommend keeping it to a paragraph or two.

I like to give a short summary of what the video is all about, being sure to include my target keywords. This gives you a slight edge when it comes to ranking the video.

Underneath the description, I like to put links for my main lead magnets, along with my paid products. So for example, if I'm uploading a video which is about starting an online business, I'll include a link to my free webinar which teaches people about online business, along with a link to The Online Business Blueprint, which is my full step-by-step program. This way, people can decide themselves what they want, whether it's a free training or a premium product. Regardless, it's important to actually have something in the description which allows you to monetise — as you can't make any money if you only describe what's in the video!

VIDEO TAGS

'Tags' are keywords which you can add to your video in order to let YouTube know what topics your video is associated to. With the title and description, you want to include your exact keyword — but with tags, you want to include 'similar' search terms.

It's important to point out that you don't want to add as many tags as you possibly can. YouTube can actually penalise you for doing this. You get 500 characters to use, and you should add as many as is necessary in order to describe what your video is about.

For example, if your main keyword is 'online business', then your tags may consist of keywords such as 'start an online business, how to start an online business, online business tips' and things like that. Don't go adding a ton of irrelevant tags.

THUMBNAILS

The thumbnail is the image that people see when scrolling through their search results. An attractive thumbnail can increase the likelihood of a person clicking on your video instead of scrolling past it. YouTube has revealed that over 90% of the best performing videos on the platform have a custom thumbnail.

In order to have a custom thumbnail, you will need to verify your YouTube account. Simply go to YouTube.com/verify and you'll be able to get it sorted.

There are a couple of different ways you can make thumbnails. If you want to do it yourself when starting out, you can go to Canva.com and use their simply drag-and-drop interface in order to make pretty cool looking thumbnails.

If you'd rather spend a few dollars and save your time, you can go to Fiverr.com and simply put 'YouTube thumbnails' in the search bar and you'll find tons of designers that can make professional-looking thumbnails for you.

END SCREEN

You know when you get to the end of a video and it shows you other videos that you can watch next? That's called an end screen. It's something that you can set up during the process of uploading your videos.

End screens are generally just a really cool way of keeping people on your channel. Remember what I said earlier about retention? Well, YouTube rewards people for keeping them on the platform — not just on a single video. If you have your end screens set up nicely, you can get people to binge on several of your videos all at one time — which works wonders for YouTube's algorithm.

I'd recommend having your end screen set to show two videos and a 'subscribe' button. This can be done very easily by just choosing a template. It's a good idea to have one link to your most recent video and the other linking to one of your all-time most popular videos.

SHARING YOUR VIDEO

Once your video is uploaded and ready to go, it's important that you get it out to the world as quickly as possible. YouTube have stated that the first 24 hours after a video is published are crucial when it comes to ranking. So this means you have one day to share the video everywhere you possibly can.

Now, while you don't want to be spamming people left, right and centre, you do want to make sure you utilise whichever platforms you can. If you publish a YouTube video, you definitely want to be sharing it with your email list, and also on Facebook. This is a no-brainer!

Once you've done all of these things, you're going to be in good stead in terms of maximising the potential of the YouTube platform. But we still have a couple more that we're going to be using, remember?

YOUR FACEBOOK PROFILE: INTIMACY AT ITS FINEST

As of April 2019, Facebook has 2.4 BILLION active monthly users. Not 2.4 billion accounts... 2.4 billion people who actually use the platform on a regular basis. So it makes sense for us to take a little piece of that pie, right?

Facebook is an awesome platform for pretty much any niche because it allows you to engage with your audience on a very intimate basis which can't quite be achieved on any other platform. Instagram's comments feature works but it's not the cleanest, and YouTube comments are the same. Facebook, however, enables you to have full-blown conversations with multiple people almost seamlessly.

Facebook profiles have a friend limit of 5,000 people. This isn't ideal if we're thinking long-term, but for the first year or two of building your business, that's plenty of people to build a relationship with. A Facebook friend is going to be far more 'valuable' relationship-wise than an Instagram or Twitter follower.

Also, another awesome thing about Facebook profiles is that the organic reach is awesome. 5,000 people might not sound like a crazy number, but a huge portion of those people will see your content when you post it. This is awesome when compared to a business page, where as little as 2% of followers will see your posts.

In terms of your actual marketing strategy with your Facebook profile, you want to focus on providing value most of the time. Like I said earlier in the book — you want to focus 80% on providing value and 20% on selling your product.

To make sure we get the most out of the platform, it's important to post regularly. If there's one way to ensure that not many people see your posts, it's to post erratically and inconsistently. The algorithm works both ways; it looks carefully at which content is interesting for other people, but it also looks for the stuff that isn't. If you only post on your Facebook profile once or twice a month, they will assume that you're not a regular poster and that nobody is really interested in your content. When this happens, you'll notice your reach and engagement will plummet.

The safest solution? Post every day. If you post every day on Facebook, you'll notice two positives: you'll be favoured by the algorithm and your reach and engagement will continually increase, and you'll also build an extremely strong relationship with your audience — far greater than you would if you were posting once per week. Because of this, you will make far more money, too.

Along with posting daily on your feed with valuable information, you should also be doing live videos. Facebook Live is a feature which is heavily favoured by the platform at the moment and they love it when people get on camera and start shooting. This is one for you camera-shy people out there — grab the camera and go live!

I would recommend going live twice a week if you can. Do it consistently on the same days every week, too. Once you schedule your live streams into your calendar, you know you're going to remember them and you'll get them done. Then, just focus on one topic which will help your audience and speak about it for 10 minutes or so. Don't overthink it!

Now that we've covered your Facebook profile, let's talk about the final element of the YPG method: Facebook groups.

FACEBOOK GROUPS: THE ULTIMATE ENGAGED COMMUNITY

Facebook groups are awesome because they're often large communities of people who are all heavily interested in the same thing. It's a super-condensed crowd of people who are all readily prepared to consume your content.

You ultimately want to have your own Facebook group but of course, you need to engage with people to begin with in order to make that happen. For this reason, it's a good idea to start out by engaging in other people's Facebook groups.

Regardless of what niche you're in, I can guarantee you won't have any difficulty finding four or five groups with tens of thousands of members each. This opens up a huge audience of people for you to build rapport with, with pretty much no effort required at all.

I always recommend that when starting out, you should spend at least 30 minutes per day simply providing value to people in Facebook groups. I just sort the posts by 'most recent' and then answer everything which has been posted in the past 24 hours. Then at the same time the following day, I do the same thing.

Then, every time somebody engages with me or I help someone, I will add them as a friend on my profile. Now, I'm able to communicate with them every day through my content.

Another really cool thing about groups is that you're not only seen by the person you help. You might be answering one person's question, but your value-packed answer might be seen by 500 other people. This leads to a barrage of friend requests from people who are interested in your topic — also known as potential buyers!

As soon as you have a few hundred friends (which won't take long), you want to set up your own Facebook group. Over the long term, you want to build the biggest audience you possibly can, and Facebook groups are an incredible way to do this.

Ideally, what you want to do is this: engage in other people's already-large Facebook groups to begin with, while adding everybody you meet. Then create your own Facebook group, and invite all of those people to your Facebook group, too. Continue engaging in the larger groups and moving their members into your own group until, eventually, your group will begin to grow by itself.

When you get a couple thousand people into your Facebook group, you can begin focusing on your own group rather than other groups. You want to focus on doing the exact same thing as you do on your profile — providing value to your audience and engaging with them. The beauty of a Facebook group is that there's no limit to the number of members. There are literally groups out there with over 1 million members... can you imagine how much money you could make if you have a million people all interested in your topic?!

Inside your group, I would recommend uploading a video and pinning it to the top of the group. Just shoot a quick 1-2 minute clip where you introduce yourself, welcome people to the group and give people an idea of what they should expect to get from the group. This is also a great time to encourage people to engage with everybody and perhaps drop a message introducing themselves. The more people engage with each other, the greater the 'community' feel.

There's also a group 'description' which you should fill out. It's an area of text where you can put pretty much whatever you want. Similar to the welcome video, you should welcome people to the group and let them know what to expect. It's also recommended that you lay down some rules and guidelines — if you don't want people promoting business opportunities in your group or selling products, it's crucial that you let everybody know this.

Here's a pro tip: in your welcome video, make sure you tell people that they need to read the description. Then, in the description, you can send people to one of your lead magnets or webinars. Voila! You've now got that person on your email list and can send them through an email sequence.

SELLING ON AUTOPILOT

HOW TO SELL YOUR PRODUCT TWENTY-FOUR HOURS A DAY

So now that we know how to actually utilise the three platforms in order to build an audience, I want to explain how you can set up systems that will sell your products on autopilot for you. These systems are called sales funnels.

Sure, it's awesome to engage with people all day long and talk them into buying your products, but that's not an efficient way to do it. You want to engage with people in order to build your audience, but you don't want to have you manually sell each person on your product. That's not scalable.

What you want to do is set up what's called a 'sales funnel' which will do all of the selling for you. All you need to do is get the person to enter the sales funnel by clicking on a link, and the rest of the work is done for you. A sales funnel is designed to take people from 'curious' to knowing, liking and trusting you, and eventually buying from you.

You don't even need to speak to each individual in order to get them to do this - a lot of the time, people will enter your sales funnels through a YouTube video or a Facebook post. This allows us to leverage our time and energy; we post something once and get multitudes of people entering into our sales funnels and buying our products.

Here's an example of a very basic sales funnel, which I've aptly called the 'Basic Funnel':

BASIC FUNNEL

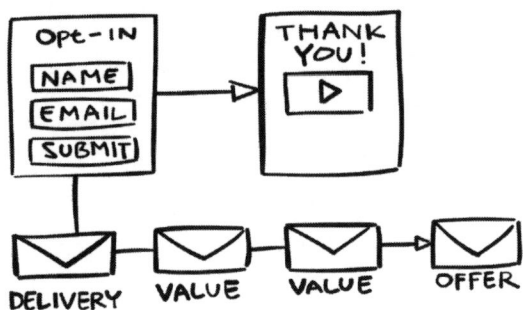

As you can see, it all starts with the 'opt-in' page. This is the page that you need to send people to. What we do here is ask people for their email address in exchange for something free. This is called a 'lead magnet' for exactly that reason — it attracts leads.

A lead is when somebody enters their details and we manage to capture their email address. They become a lead. We can now market to them and eventually, turn that lead into a customer. That's all business is about; acquiring leads and turning them into customers.

After they enter their details, we send people to a 'thank you' page. A lot of people try and sell something on this page, but I've found that this isn't necessarily the best way to go about things. It's a quick way to kill rapport and that's definitely not something we want.

I personally find that the 'thank you' page is the perfect place to insert a quick 60-90 second video just thanking them for showing an interest in your free gift and letting them know that they should expect a ton of value from you over the next few days.

Once the person opts in to receive our free gift (lead magnet), we're now legally allowed to market to them until they unsubscribe or tell us to stop. Most people don't unsubscribe and you're able to sell to them for years on end. Some people, however, will unsubscribe. And that's absolutely fine. If people don't want to see our content, we don't want to contact them anyway.

Now, the goal is to get them to buy something. If we can make more money selling things to our leads than it costs to acquire them, we're running a profitable business. And using the tactics that I've outlined inside this book, we're not paying anything to acquire them — so we're starting in a pretty awesome position!

I want to let you in on another secret that marketers use to make massive profits within their business...

Autoresponders.

You see in the basic funnel diagram, where the person opts in and goes through to the 'thank you' page? Well, they also receive ongoing emails where we can provide value to them and sell them stuff.

The key here is that you don't want to be sending all of these emails manually, as that takes up time. What we want here is leverage. There's that word again... leverage.

What we can do is, before we even send anybody to the opt-in page, we can set up a series of emails which will go out to all of your leads on complete autopilot, on a schedule that we choose ahead of time. This is called an 'autoresponder sequence' or more commonly, an email sequence.

This allows us to get more 'bang for our buck' when it comes to writing out emails — we write them once and then they're all automatically sent to every single person who comes into our funnel. I've literally spent three hours writing out an email sequence before and it's led to over 50,000 emails being sent on complete autopilot. Crazy!

The way that we set up an email sequence is by using email software programs that are made specifically for this. There are tons of different programs you can use: Aweber, ConvertKit, ActiveCampaign, GetResponse, MailChimp... the list goes on.

I would actually recommend using Actionetics, which is the built-in email marketing feature that comes with ClickFunnels — which happens to be the program we use to build our sales funnels too so we kill two birds with one stone. The reason I like Actionetics is because it allows us to track how much revenue each email has generated for us.

This is incredibly useful for us because if we have this information, we can actually reverse-engineer the numbers and figure out how much each lead is worth to us. Then, we simply go out and get leads for less than that number. If we know that each lead is worth $10, we can buy leads for $5 all day long knowing for certain that we're profitable.

Anyway, I'm going off-topic but that's the gist of how a sales funnel works. We bring the person to the opt-in page, capture their email address and then send them through a sequence of valuable emails which sell our stuff to them. It's important that you always focus on value in your email sequences, otherwise people will unsubscribe. It doesn't matter how 'automated' or 'hands-off' your systems are if people aren't interested, right?

What I'd like to do is show you a few more sales funnels that you can use to promote your products. The basic funnel that I just explained to you is definitely good enough to generate a profit, especially when you're first starting out, but there are some other types of funnels which can generate a LOT more money when executed correctly.

VIDEO SERIES FUNNEL

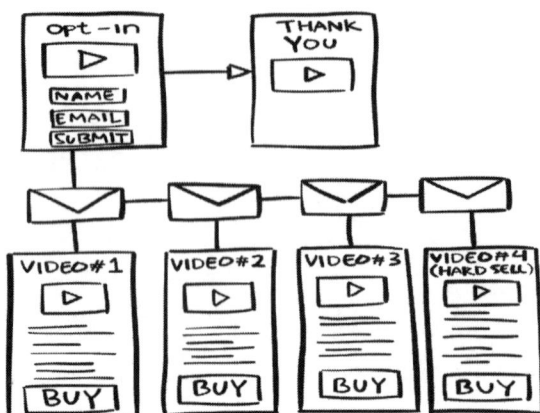

The video series funnel is a step up from the basic funnel. It has the potential to be more profitable and gives the prospect more opportunities to buy from you.

The cool thing about this funnel is that the actual funnel itself is the lead magnet. Instead of just delivering an eBook or cheatsheet to somebody via email, we send them through a mini-course consisting of video trainings, which are placed on individual funnel pages.

So when they opt in, we send them an automated email which sends them to lesson one. Then, on the second day, they get another automated email which sends them to lesson two. And this can last from anywhere from 3 to 5 days. I personally find that 4 days is the sweet spot.

When they're going through this mini-course, they end up knowing, liking and trusting us far more than they would if they simply read an eBook or something like that. It allows us to build much more rapport with the lead.

Not only this, but it gives us more opportunities to make money. In each of these videos, you can provide a ton of value and then mention your product. I'd recommend taking it easy, though — only do a 'hard sell' (where you really tell them to buy) at the end of the final video in the course. In the other videos, I just briefly mention that I have a program and they can scroll down below the page to check it out if they're interested.

That brings me to my next point. With the video series funnel, an awesome little tactic you can use is to put a mini version of your sales page below each of the mini-course videos. So instead of sending people to a page that literally just has a training video on it, you send them to a page which has a training video and then a mini-sales letter underneath it. Then a button at the bottom of the screen which sends the person to your main sales page. This means that there's a chance of somebody buying every single time they watch one of the videos in the series.

The goal with this funnel is to build huge amounts of rapport with the prospect, but also to actually get them to buy the product. We want it to be a 'self-liquidating' funnel which means that if you're spending money on advertising, the money you make from the person going through the video series covers what you spend. Then you've essentially acquired a free lead.

The money-making doesn't stop at the end of the mini-course though. You want to continue sending the person emails to maximise the potential profit of the lead. Every time you bring out some content (I'm mainly talking YouTube videos here), you should compose an email pointing to that video and add it on to the end of your email sequence. So eventually you'll have 3-5 videos which send people to the mini-course but then you might have 60, 90 or even 120 days of emails which send people to your pure 'value' content.

And remember... every single one of your YouTube videos is going to have your product linked in the description. Get it? Sooner or later, a lot of people are going to make the decision to buy.

THE WEBINAR FUNNEL

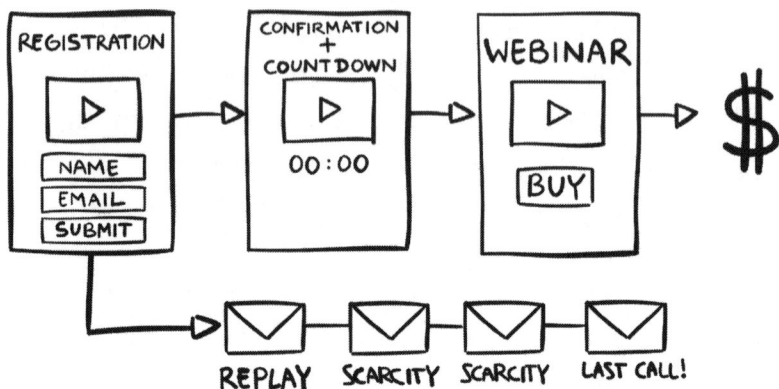

The webinar funnel is one of my all-time favourite funnels. It allows you to make money from leads and acquire potential customers very quickly. Within an hour or so, in fact.

The video series funnel might take a few days to get people to pull out their card and buy, whereas a webinar gets people to buy right there on the spot. The idea of a webinar is to provide as much value as possible for 40-60 minutes, building up such a high level of trust that people are willing to buy instantly.

While a basic funnel or a video series funnel might work well for products at lower price-points, webinar funnels work incredibly well for anything priced from $300 to around $2,000. This is why it's one of my favourite funnels for selling an online course.

As you can see, we send people to an opt-in page, similar to the opt-in page for the other funnels. Then, once the person opts in, they go through to a 'countdown' page which will redirect the person to the webinar once it begins. You can set your webinar up inside ClickFunnels to play as frequently as you like; every day, every hour, every 10 minutes and so on. I like to set it up to play every 10 minutes as it means people don't have to wait on the countdown page for long.

Once the countdown timer hits zero, the person is redirected to the webinar which will play as soon as they click on the video. It's important to make sure the webinar has no control buttons (this can easily be set up in Vimeo or Wistia, where you host the video) because this way, people can skip through the video before you've provided any value and see your pitch — and this will pretty much kill your chances of making a sale.

You want to provide a ton of value to the prospect, but it's also crucial that you eliminate any limiting beliefs regarding whatever it is you're selling. One of the main things that will stop a person from investing in a product or course is that they don't think that it will work for them. You have to get rid of any obstacles and objections that they may have, and show tons of social proof — testimonials and reviews etc. — to help them feel as confident in the product as possible.

I recommend setting the first email in your sequence to be a 'replay' email, directing people who missed the training to go and check it out again. This time, however, just send them straight to the webinar page, not the countdown page. This will generally bring you an extra 5-10% in revenue from the people who were distracted from the initial viewing.

After the first email, I always recommend having a series of scarcity emails which push quite a hard sale. I like to do a 4 or 5-day sequence which contains tons of testimonials, social proof and urgency. The key here is to take something away if people don't purchase your product by the end of the 5 days.

Then, at the end of the five days, you take something away, for example the price might go up or you can remove some (or all) of the free bonuses.

Of course, as with every other funnel, this isn't the end of the marketing process. We're hoping to at least break even or even be profitable by the end of the 5-day urgency sequence but either way, we still want to continue marketing to these people. For this reason, I'd recommend adding value videos onto the end of the sequence and building it out nice and long. These videos should be less salesy but still direct people to your content where they may end up choosing to buy.

FREE + SHIPPING BOOK FUNNEL

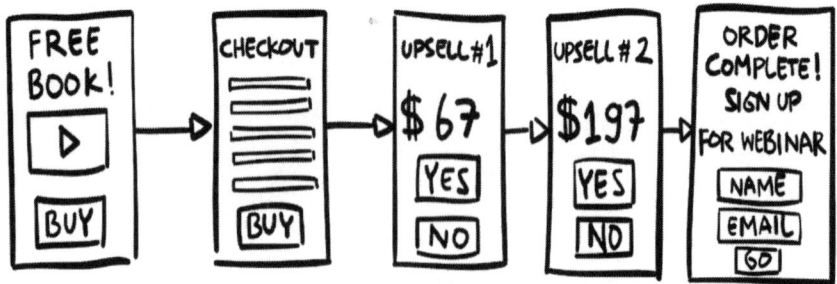

This is a more complex funnel, but it's one of my all-time favourites. The main reason for this is because it generates tons of qualified buyers — people who have proven that they're ready to pull out their credit card and spend money.

If you want to see a perfect example of what a free book funnel looks like, think back to when you purchased this book... because you went through one! That's right — I'm sharing the secret sauce with you. I'm literally going to explain the exact marketing tactics that I'm using to sell this book to my audience. Perhaps you'll be able to go out and get people to buy your 'free + shipping' offer exactly the same way that I got you to buy mine.

The main idea of a free + shipping funnel is to liquidate your costs. Remember what that means? It means that we want to make enough money on the 'front end' that all of our costs, whether it's the cost of the product (in my case, a book) or any money you spend on ads have been completely recouped and you've gained a customer for free.

For this reason, what a lot of people do is position the book as a 'free' offer but then charge for the shipping. Depending on the production/fulfilment cost of the book you're giving away, this may be $5, it may be $10 or it may be $15 shipping. I can't tell you what's right or wrong — you need to figure it out yourself.

For example, in my case, I might charge $10 for shipping. So if the book itself costs me $5 to print and deliver, I'm left with another $5 that I can spend on ads in order to make a sale. If I can acquire a customer and ship the book for less than $10, I've essentially made my money back and the new customer hasn't cost me anything. If it costs me more than $10 to make the sale and ship the book, I'm going to lose money each time I make the sale. So how do I combat this?

Upsells.

Upsells are absolutely incredible. Without upsells, a free + shipping funnel is only going to generate, let's say, $10 (revenue, not profit) per customer. So if it's costing us $10 to make the sale, we're not making any money. However, once you add some valuable upsells that people can buy after the purchase, we can increase each sale to $20, $30 or even $40 per customer.

So, as opposed to beforehand when we could only spend $10 to sell a copy of the book, we can now potentially spend 20, 30 or even 40 bucks to acquire a customer. It's a LOT easier to get somebody to buy a free book when you've got $40 to spend than it is with $10 to spend.

This makes it incredibly easy for us to make the funnel profitable and everything you sell to them after the initial sale is pure profit. And like I said earlier, these people are super keen on buying because they proved it by buying the book in the first place. This isn't always the case with a freebie or a mini-course.

When you're creating upsells to add onto your book funnel, I recommend creating video courses. The free offer itself can be a book, but if you're going to add upsells, we want something of higher perceived value. Video courses can be great for this because we can price them at $50 all the way up to $300, which means that we can really bump up that average cart value.

You don't want to add a bunch of $5 upsells because that way, even if people do purchase them, it's not going to really bump your average cart value up much. I'd recommend having at least two upsells when people buy the book — a video training course prices at around $67 and then another video training course which teaches a different aspect of the subject, prices at around $197. These two price points will allow you to really bump up that average order value so that you can make the funnel profitable.

Another important thing to note is that you want to make sure your upsells are one-click upsells. What I mean by this is that once somebody has purchased the book, you don't want them to have to put their card details in again in order to purchase the upsells. This will destroy the conversion rate of your upsells. I'm not going to explain how to set all of this up (you can't really explain it in a book) but a one-click upsell will allow you to do just that — upsell people with one click. When somebody enters their credit card details and buys your book, the order is held open momentarily while they're offered the upsells.

If they click 'no' on the upsell, it'll simply take them to the next one. If they click 'yes' on the upsell, it will add the product to their order and take them to the next one. Then, once they've been through all the upsells (usually two or three) it will automatically complete the order based on whatever they've chosen. So they only entered their card details when buying the book, but if they've clicked 'yes' on the upsells then they'll be billed for those too. This means that your upsells can convert pretty damn well!

Another really cool pro tip that you can use is this — once your customer has purchased the free book and they've been through all the upsells, you can instantly redirect them to your webinar! How clever is that? Then, even though you've already made money from them, they can now go straight through to your 'free training' and potentially buy your high-ticket product.

And as long as the book and the upsells are in place, you should already be profitable; which means that every single high-ticket sale you make from your webinar viewers will be 100% profit — insane!

Once again, this works like every other funnel in the sense that once people have purchased the book and the upsells, we still want to continually market to them on an ongoing basis. And this is all profit, too.

DELIVERY - THE SECRET TO SCALING!

DELIVERY AUTOMATION IS KEY

Now that we know how to build an audience and we know how to actually sell our product to them, I want to touch on another topic which really catches a lot of business owners out, especially in the online space.

Getting people's attention is easy, all it takes is good content and consistency. Putting systems in place to indoctrinate these people and sell your product, well that's not hard either. It takes some practice and some knowledge but it's doable. But this third point. This one can be a killer.

In order to scale your business, you must make sure that the overall delivery of your product is scalable. So many business owners build their entire business and then get caught by this. If the actual delivery of your product isn't scalable, your entire business will grind to a halt and you'll be left wondering why.

As I mentioned at the very beginning of this book, I first started out in business by running advertising for clients. I did everything myself on the technical side — I didn't have a team or anything. Before long, I found that the more clients I signed, the more work was required. This wasn't an issue for me because I didn't push the business model to its limits; I was looking for more of a 'lifestyle' business. But if I did try and take it as far as I could, I knew I'd eventually reach a point where I literally ran out of time and couldn't take on any more clients.

This applies to pretty much every business model where you're exchanging time for money. Any service-based business is eventually going to plateau because you can't acquire more time or energy. One-on-one coaching, done-for-you services, consulting... they will all eventually plateau.

So if this was the case, how could I combat this problem? How could I create a business which wasn't hindered by time, and would continue to grow larger and larger without me having to put in any extra work?

I created an online course.

That's the beauty of an online course business — as you make more and more sales, the efficiency of the business isn't affected and the customer experience isn't affected. If anything, it actually gets better. The reason for this is because as you gain more and more customers, you can get a ton of feedback and actually improve the product.

With a consulting business for example, once you get to a certain number of clients, the level of service you're able to offer is going to deteriorate. You're going to be able to give far more attention to your clients if you have 5 of them than you would if you had 50 of them. That's just the way done-for-you businesses and one-on-one businesses work. This isn't an issue with an online course business.

In your online course business, you want to create systems which literally automate everything. Systems are the key to scaling your business in the long term without any extra effort. I literally think of ways to automate every single little thing in my business so that it's completely hands-off.

For example, when somebody buys your online course, you don't want to have to contact them personally to give them access to the program. So what you can do is set up a delivery email which is completely automated so that every time somebody purchases the course, they receive an email with a unique link where they can create their account and log in.

But on top of that, I want to make sure that all students have access to the private Facebook community, so instead of having to invite them myself, I make sure I give them a link to the group and clear directions on how to join. But you can take it a step further — every time somebody signs up to one of my programs, I also include an affiliate sign-up link in the delivery email so that if they choose to do so, they can actually sign up as an affiliate and promote the course in exchange for 40% commission. This is an incredibly effective way of making more money and it's literally an effortless way to get all of your new customers to begin promoting your products right off the bat.

Usually, you'll have customers message you every now and then asking about your affiliate program. Then, you need to go and get a link, send it through to them and explain how it all works. When you include this in the onboarding email, it removes that work entirely. These are all little automated 'systems' that I love putting in place that allow me to increase my profits without having to put in any extra effort whatsoever.

You want to figure out ways of automating every single part of your business that you possibly can. Remember, you don't want to compromise on the efficiency or effectiveness of the product. If something is going to ruin the customer experience in any way, it probably shouldn't be automated. But if it can simply take a job off your hands and machine-ize (is that even a word?) it, you should absolutely be aiming to automate it.

What you're aiming for in the long run is to be solely focusing on creating content and improving your product. You want your traffic to be automated through past content and paid ads (once you go down that route, even if it's just retargeting), your actual conversion process should be automated through a sales funnel with a lengthy, effective follow-up sequence, and the entire 'value delivery' process should be automated, with the entirety of the product and anything else the customer needs being delivered through an email leading to an online course. Once you're in this position, you won't believe how easy things become, and you'll suddenly realise that you're able to truly live that 'laptop lifestyle' that everybody desperately wants.

CONCLUSION

CONCLUSION

Wow, we're at the end of the book already! That was an absolute blast.

We've covered some incredibly useful topics which are going to make your life a hell of a lot easier when trying to get your business off the ground. Simply by putting the information in this book into practice, you're going to avoid a lot of the mistakes that I made when I first started.

We all learn from mistakes — but they don't have to be your mistakes. A wise man looks at the mistakes of others and learns from them, in order to avoid making those mistakes altogether. When I first started out, I made a lot of mistakes and I wasted a lot of time trying to find valuable resources which would teach me how to start an online business. I was scrolling through countless YouTube videos, I was looking inside Facebook groups and I was buying courses left and right. The problem was, I didn't know what information was good and what information was garbage. Unfortunately for me, I realised after a while that 95% of it is garbage.

This was the exact reason that I decided to write Fire Your Boss. I've had countless people asking me for recommendations of good marketing books and the truth is, there are very few. There are tons of books which talk about theory; 300-page books which could easily be condensed to 20 pages — and nobody wants to read those.

But in terms of actual steps to take, I couldn't really find anything decent. So I thought why not write a book and outline some of the strategies that I use so that other people can benefit from them — and the feedback has been phenomenal.

But the learning doesn't stop with this book. In fact, we're only just getting started. If you've watched any of my content or been following my social media channels, you'll know that I have a step-by-step program called The Online Business Blueprint which teaches *everything* you need to know about this business model. It consists of in-depth training on all aspects of online business: building your audience, creating your product, setting up your sales funnels, launching your product in the most efficient way, and lots more. The information included in The Online Business Blueprint has cost me literally tens of thousands of dollars to gather, through high-ticket coaching from some of the best names in the business. But now, it's all packaged up in one place, ready for you to begin implementing straight away — The Online Business Blueprint.

Not only that, but all students who join get access to personal mentorship from me inside our student community and also through Facebook Messenger, where I'm able to guide and advise you through the use of voice notes.

In fact, I'd invite you to join The Online Business Blueprint. If you've found this book to be valuable and you'd like to further your learning on the subject in order to really kick-start your online course business, I'd like to invite you to go ahead and visit the program at ryansblueprint.com to learn more.

I hope you've enjoyed reading this book as much as I've enjoyed writing it. If you take action on what you've learned, you won't believe the progress you can make in both your business and in your life. You've got the tools, now it's time to make it happen.

Be sure to keep in touch on social media and let me know about your successes along the way!

Ryan Wegner
Creator of The Online Business Blueprint™